D0630396

SOPHOPHOBIA IS
THE FEAR OF
LEARNING
LEARN
SOMETHING
EVERY DAY

RINGO TRANSLATES AS "APPLE" IN JAPANESE

RIGHT-HANDED
PEOPLE LIVE LONGER
THAN LEFT-HANDED PEOPLE

CHARLIE CHAPLIN ONCE CAME IN THIRD IN A CHAPLIN LOOKALIKE CONTEST

ONE SMALL STEP FOR MAN...
ONE GIANT LEAK FOR MANKIND...
ASTRONAUTS WEAR DIAPERS

CATS SLEEP FOR 70% OF THEIR LIVES

EMERSON MOSER, CRAYOLA'S SENIOR CRAYON MAKER, REVEALED AT RETIREMENT THAT HE WAS COLOR-BLIND

THE ANGLO-ZANZIBAR WAR WAS THE SHORTEST AT JUST 38 MINUTES

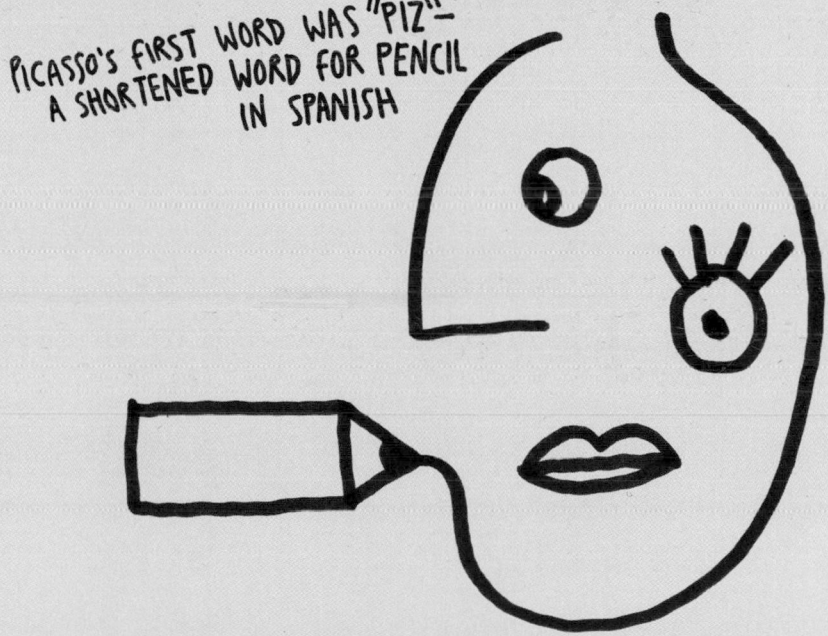
PICASSO'S FIRST WORD WAS "PIZ"–
A SHORTENED WORD FOR PENCIL
IN SPANISH

ELEPHANTS
CAN'T
JUMP

DAVID BOWIE HAS A SPIDER SPECIES NAMED AFTER HIM

ELVIS WAS NATURALLY BLOND

WAYNE ALLWINE, THE VOICE OF MICKEY MOUSE, WAS MARRIED TO RUSSI TAYLOR, THE VOICE OF MINNIE

PIGS DON'T SWEAT

A PEANUT IS NOT A NUT

OWLS CAN'T MOVE THEIR EYES

THERE WAS NO
"MID SEPTEMBER"
IN 1752

IT WOULD TAKE 30 YEARS TO COUNT TO ONE BILLION

A LONG GAME OF HIDE AND SEEK

THE LONGEST BEARD WAS JUST OVER 6 FEET LONG

NEANDERTHALS HAD BIGGER BRAINS THAN HUMANS

SOME
WHALES
COMMIT
SUICIDE

PIGS CAN'T LOOK UP
AT THE SKY

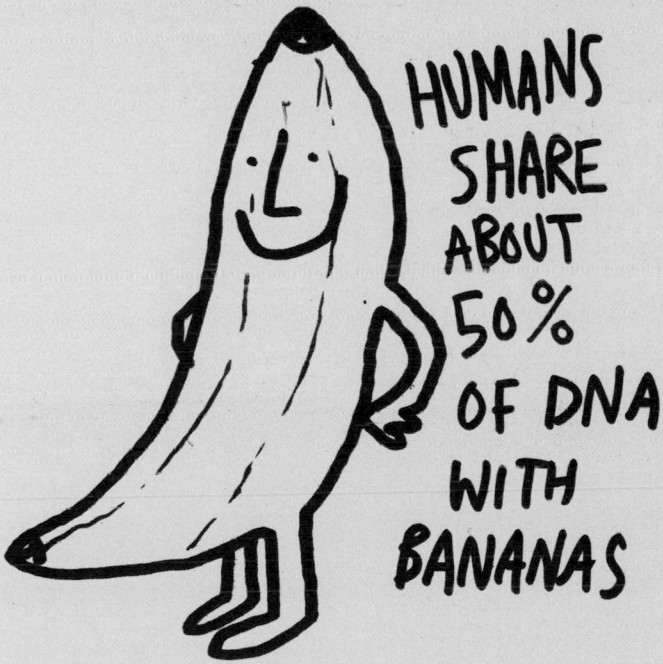
HUMANS SHARE ABOUT 50% OF DNA WITH BANANAS

THOMAS EDISON,
INVENTOR OF
THE LIGHTBULB,
WAS SCARED
OF THE DARK

PENGUINS ARE ABLE TO JUMP 6·5 FEET HIGH

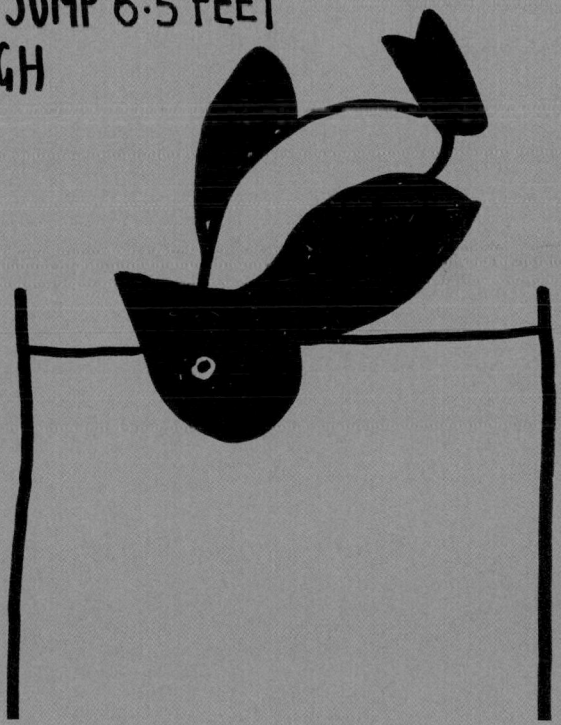

STARFISH HAVE NO BRAINS

STAR PUPIL

JIM HENSON DEVELOPED AN ALLERGY TO FLEECE

THE AVERAGE WORKER HONEYBEE MAKES ONLY 1/12 TEASPOON DURING HIS LIFETIME

A PIG'S
WILLY
IS
SHAPED
LIKE A
CORKSCREW

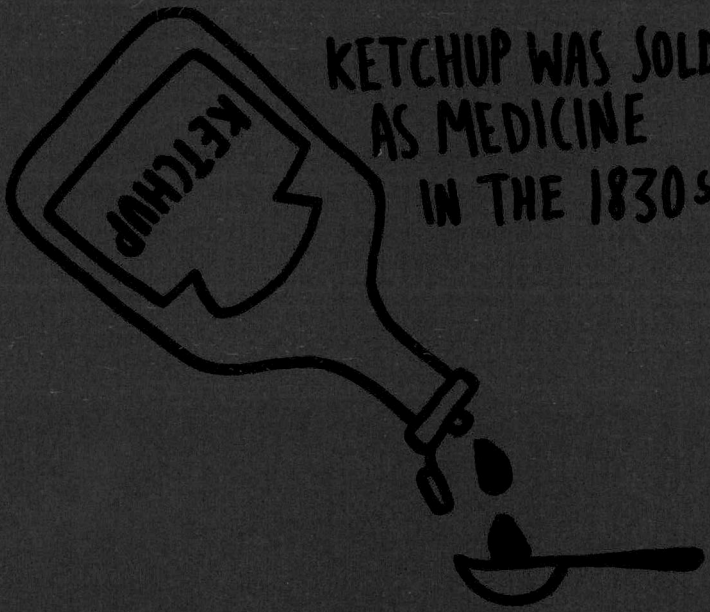

KETCHUP WAS SOLD AS MEDICINE IN THE 1830s

COWS CAN
GO UP STAIRS
BUT NOT
DOWN

WOMEN CRY 4
TIMES AS OFTEN
AS MEN

JOHN LENNON'S CAT WAS CALLED ELVIS

MUHAMMAD ALI HAS AN IQ OF 78
FLOAT LIKE A BUTTERFLY STING LIKE... ERM...

A CHICKEN SURVIVED 18 MONTHS WITHOUT A HEAD

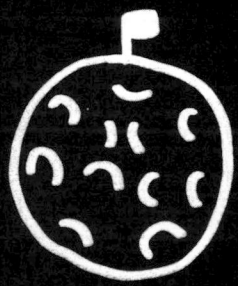

GOLF IS THE ONLY SPORT TO BE PLAYED ON THE MOON

WOMEN BLINK
NEARLY TWICE AS
OFTEN AS MEN

4,000-YEAR-OLD CHEESE WAS FOUND IN EGYPTIAN TOMBS

130 CUPS OF TEA
WOULD BE A LETHAL
DOSE OF CAFFEINE

ESCAPIST
HARRY HOUDINI
DIED ON HALLOWEEN

HITLER WAS
VOTED "TIME"
MAGAZINE'S
MAN OF THE YEAR
IN 1938

SWEDISH SWEET MAKER ROLAND OHISSON WAS BURIED IN A CHOCOLATE COFFIN

IN EQUAL QUANTITY A LEMON HAS MORE SUGAR THAN A STRAWBERRY
?

A DENTIST
INVENTED
THE ELECTRIC
CHAIR

ALL THE SWANS IN ENGLAND
ARE PROPERTY OF THE QUEEN

THE SOUND OF
E·T· WALKING
WAS MADE WITH
JELLY

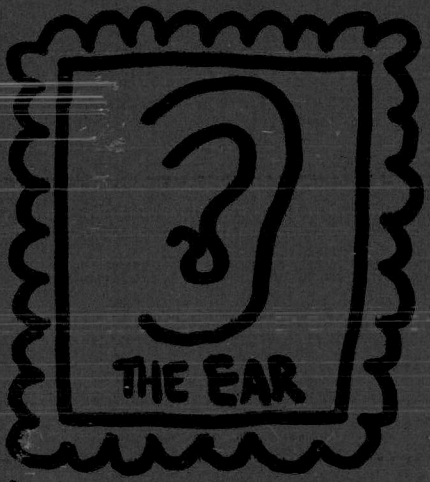

VAN GOGH ONLY SOLD ONE PAINTING DURING HIS LIFETIME

ANTS CAN LIFT
50 TIMES
THEIR WEIGHT

THE FATTEST MAN WAS
1,400 POUNDS

DAVE?
IF SHARKS GO UPSIDE DOWN THEY SLIP INTO A COMA

A HERD
OF GIRAFFES
IS CALLED
A TOWER

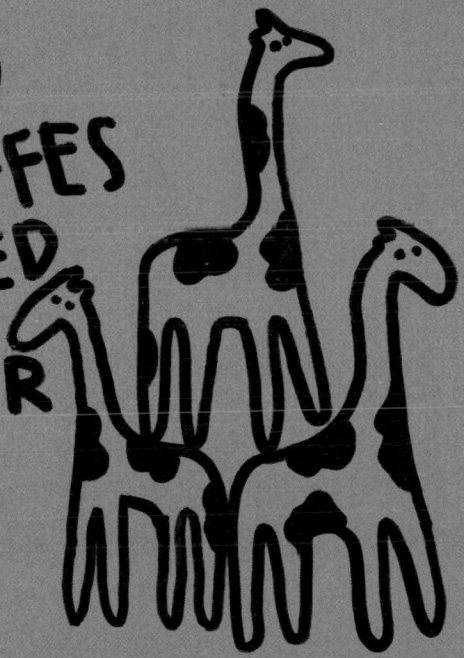

BARRY MANILOW DIDN'T WRITE HIS HIT "I WRITE THE SONGS"

THERE ARE MORE STARS IN THE SKY THAN GRAINS OF SAND ON THE EARTH

THE SPACE BETWEEN YOUR
EYEBROWS IS CALLED THE GLABELLA

KISSING FOR 1 MINUTE
CAN BURN 26 CALORIES

READING ABOUT YAWNING
WILL MAKE YOU YAWN

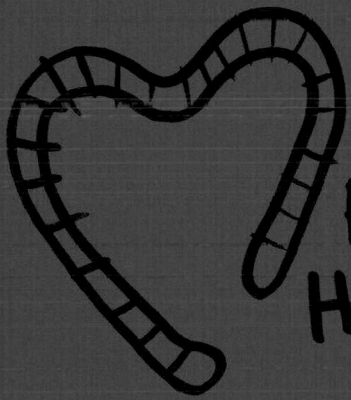

EARTHWORMS HAVE UP TO 9 HEARTS

ABBA NEVER USED THE ABBA RHYMING PATTERN

BATS
ALWAYS
TURN LEFT
WHEN EXITING
A CAVE

THE BEATLES USED THE WORD "LOVE" 613 TIMES IN THEIR SONGS

THE AVERAGE PERSON RELOCATES
11 TIMES

THE FILM "TITANIC"
COST MORE
THAN THE
TITANIC
ITSELF

THE ONLY GUY WITHOUT A BEARD IN ZZ TOP HAS THE SURNAME BEARD

THERE ARE
AROUND 61
TREES PER PERSON

THE SMALLEST
BONE IN YOUR BODY
IS IN YOUR EAR

COLUMBUS BELIEVED THE EARTH WAS PEAR SHAPED

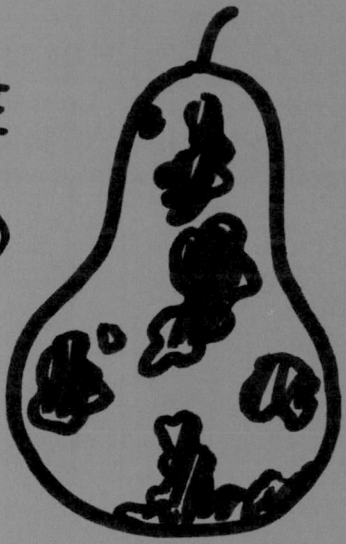

IN TEXAS IT'S
ILLEGAL TO
GRAFFITI A COW
GRAFFITI

A BLUE MOON
COMES ONCE
EVERY 2.7 YEARS

CATS CANT TASTE SWEETNESS

GOLDFISH CAN'T
CLOSE THEIR EYES

CHILDREN GROW FASTER DURING SPRING

HIPPOPOTOMONSTROS-
ESQUIPPEDALIOPHOBIA
IS THE FEAR OF
LONG WORDS

ELVIS GOT A "C" GRADE IN MUSIC CLASS
THANK YUH VERY MUCH

THE AVERAGE HUMAN BODY CONTAINS ENOUGH IRON TO MAKE A 3-INCH NAIL

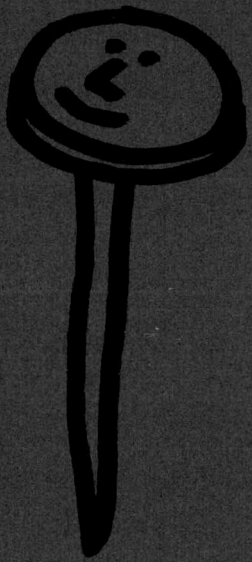

BARBIE'S FULL NAME
IS BARBARA MILLICENT
ROBERTS

THOU SHALT NOT STEAL

THE BIBLE IS THE MOST SHOPLIFTED BOOK

A RUBIK'S CUBE HAS
43,252,003,274,489,856,000
POSSIBLE COMBINATIONS

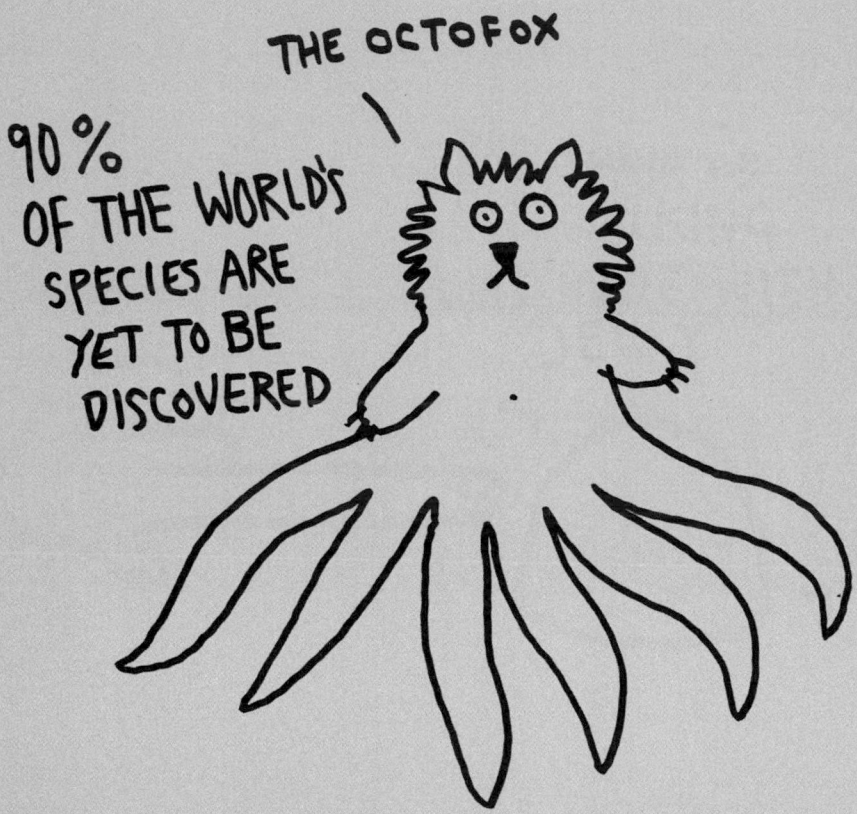
THE OCTOFOX
90%
OF THE WORLD'S
SPECIES ARE
YET TO BE
DISCOVERED

TENNIS PLAYER
VIKTOR TROICKI
IS ALLERGIC TO GRASS

THE SLOWEST
FISH IS
A SEAHORSE

LOU REED WAS GIVEN
ELECTROSHOCK TREATMENT
WHEN HE WAS YOUNG

BABOONS WERE ONCE TRAINED BY EGYPTIANS TO WAIT ON TABLES

YOU CAN'T NAME A FOLDER "CON" IN MICROSOFT WINDOWS

GIRAFFES CLEAN THEIR EARS WITH THEIR 18-INCH-LONG TONGUES

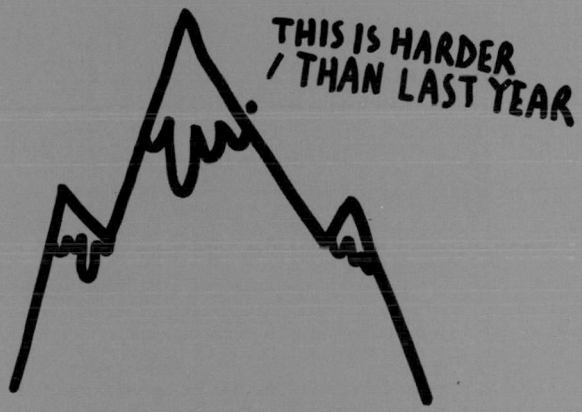

MOUNT EVEREST GROWS
1/4 INCH A YEAR

ON AVERAGE, WOMEN LIVE LONGER THAN MEN

TO LIFT A 110 POUND PERSON, YOU'LL NEED 4,000 HELIUM BALLOONS

MEN ARE MORE LIKELY TO GET STRUCK BY LIGHTNING THAN WOMEN

FROGS
DON'T
DRINK
BUD

ANCIENT EGYPTIANS THOUGHT HEDGEHOGS CURED BALDNESS

THE LONGEST BOXING MATCH LASTED 110 ROUNDS

A COWARD WAS A BOY WHO TOOK CARE OF COWS

I WANT THOSE
PARIS HILTON HAS SIZE 11 FEET

STAYING AWAKE FOR 2 WEEKS CAN KILL YOU

THE KING
OF HEARTS
IS THE ONLY
KING WITHOUT
A MUSTACHE

THE "MONA LISA" HAS NO EYEBROWS

ADULT FEET PRODUCE ¼ CUP OF SWEAT A DAY

ONE CIGARETTE
TAKES 5 MINUTES
OFF THE SMOKER'S
LIFE

95% OF PEOPLE CAN GUESS SOMEONE'S SEX JUST FROM SMELLING THEIR BREATH

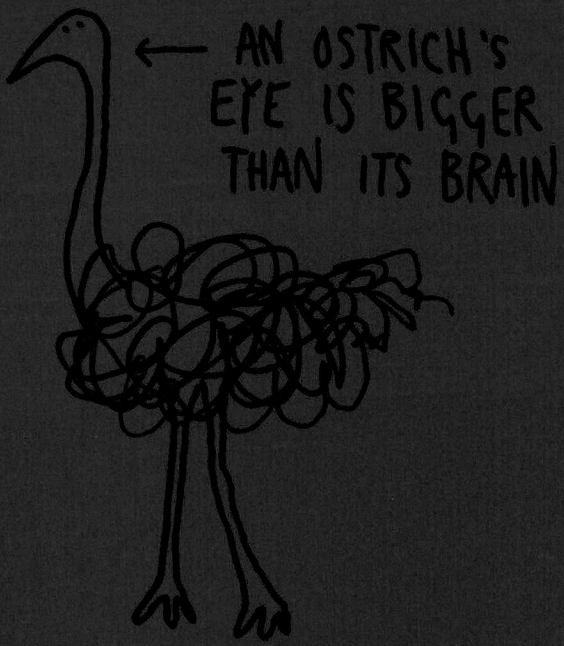
AN OSTRICH'S
EYE IS BIGGER
THAN ITS BRAIN

SHERLOCK HOLMES NEVER SAID "ELEMENTARY, MY DEAR WATSON"

BLAH
BLAH
HA
HA
CHILDREN
LAUGH UP TO
20 TIMES MORE
THAN ADULTS

POLAR BEARS HAVE BLACK SKIN
NEW HAIRCUT?

AN AVERAGE MAN SPENDS 145 DAYS OF HIS LIFE SHAVING

A BEAVER'S
TEETH
NEVER
STOP
GROWING

THE
HIGHEST
SCRABBLE
SCORE
WAS
1,049

14·4 MILLION LETTERS ARE LOST IN THE MAIL EACH YEAR

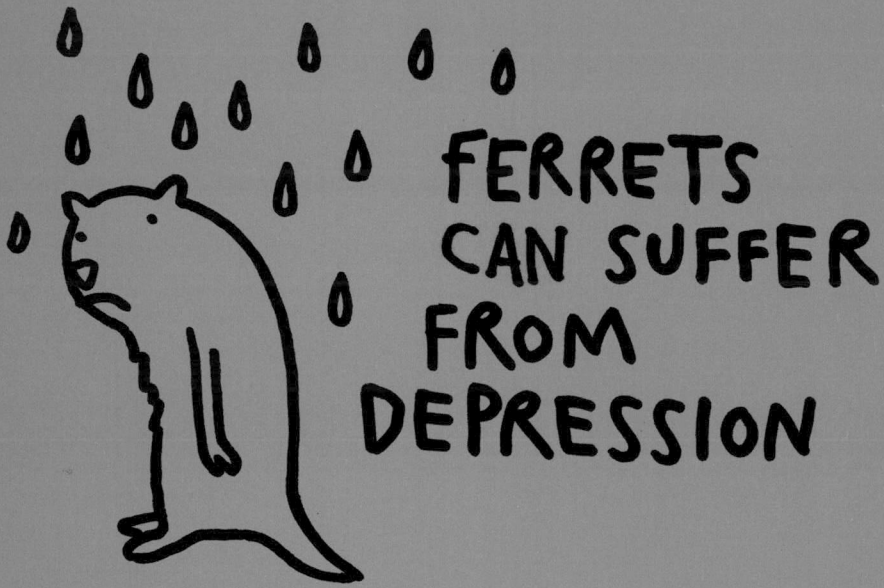
FERRETS
CAN SUFFER
FROM
DEPRESSION

A DOG'S SENSE OF SMELL IS 100 TIMES AS GOOD AS A HUMAN'S

ROARING SCHOOL

CHEETAHS CAN'T ROAR

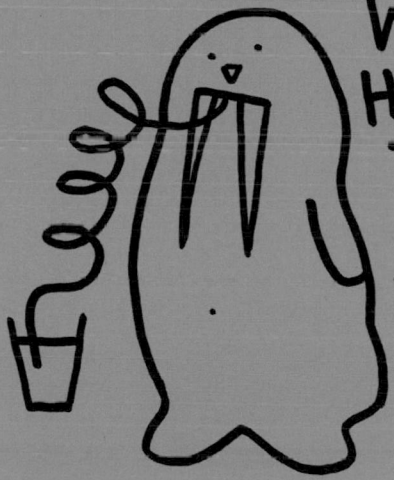

WALRUSES HAVE 3 TIMES THE SUCKING POWER OF A VACUUM CLEANER

YOU CAN
WALK ON
CUSTARD

MORE MEN THAN WOMEN TAKE TEDDY BEARS TO BED

YOUR SKULL IS MADE UP OF

BONES

NEWBORN BABIES BLINK ONLY ONCE OR TWICE A MINUTE

YOUR BODY IS MADE UP OF 66% WATER

THE HORMONE THAT MAKES YOU GROW IS PRODUCED ONLY WHEN YOU SLEEP

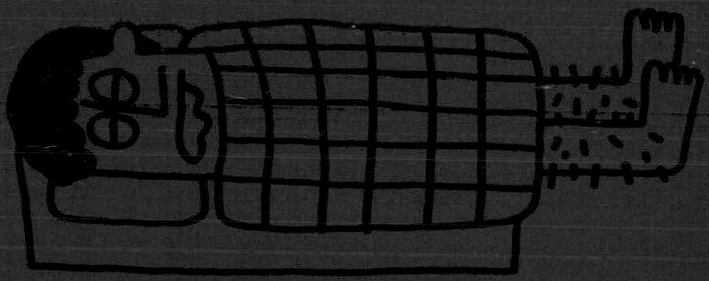

GIRAFFES FALL 6.5 FEET WHEN THEY'RE BORN

HUMANS ARE THE ONLY ANIMALS THAT CRY TEARS WHEN SAD

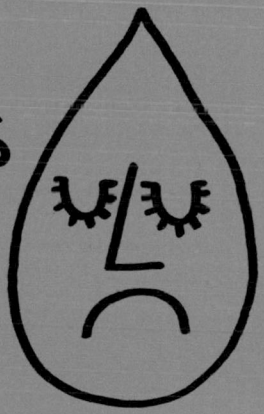

THERE IS NO SUNSHINE IN THE SOUTH POLE FOR 182 DAYS A YEAR

THE OLDEST PERSON TO GROW A TOOTH WAS 125 YEARS OLD

SCIENTISTS HAVE INVENTED GLOW-IN-THE-DARK PIGS

BILL GATES IS WEALTHIER THAN 140 NATIONS

A MOUSE'S HEART BEATS EVERY 0.009 SECONDS

A FLASH OF LIGHTNING TAKES 0.0001 SECONDS

ANTEATERS CAN EAT UP TO 30,000 ANTS A DAY

THERE'S
ENOUGH CARBON
IN YOUR BODY
TO MAKE 900
PENCILS

THE MOON IS MOVING AWAY FROM THE EARTH

ABOVE AVERAGE

THE AVERAGE HEAD GROWS 115 FEET OF HAIR A DAY

BELOW AVERAGE

WOMEN'S PUBLIC BATHROOMS CONTAIN TWICE AS MUCH BACTERIA THAN MEN'S

IN MOST HOMES, THE TOILET CONTAINS FEWER GERMS THAN THE KITCHEN

ON AVERAGE, 12 NEWBORNS WILL BE GIVEN TO THE WRONG PARENTS EVERY DAY

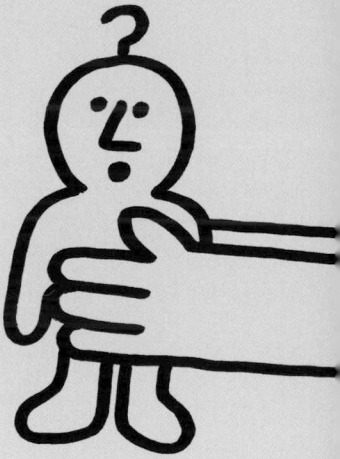

FLIES EAT BY VOMITING ON THEIR FOOD

ON AVERAGE,
A HAMSTER
WILL RUN UP TO
3 MILES A NIGHT

A CAT WOULD HAVE TO EAT 5 MICE TO GAIN THE SAME NUTRITIONAL VALUE AS A CAN OF CAT FOOD

THE OLDEST BRIDE
WAS 102

EINSTEIN COULD NEVER REMEMBER HIS PHONE NUMBER

SHAKESPEARE WAS DYSLEXIC

"SPACE INVADERS" WAS SO POPULAR IN JAPAN IT CREATED A COIN SHORTAGE

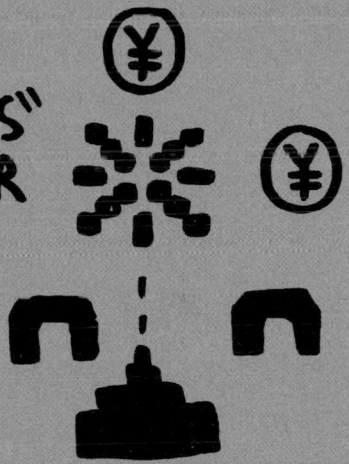

DOGS LIKE EATING
CAT POO

IT TAKES
0.0004 SECONDS
TO RETRIEVE
A MEMORY

YOU CAN MAKE DIAMONDS OUT OF DEAD PEOPLE

THE MOST HATED SOUND
IS THAT OF SOMEONE VOMITING

A SHARK CAN GROW 30,000 TEETH IN ITS LIFETIME

THE BIG BANG THEORY WAS DEVELOPED BY A PRIEST
OH GOD...

35,000 SQUARE MILES
OF FORESTS
ARE CUT DOWN
EACH YEAR

THE WOLF SPIDER CARRIES ITS YOUNG ON ITS BACK

TOXOCARA WORMS CAN EAT THROUGH A HUMAN EYEBALL

THERE ARE MORE THAN 600 SPECIES OF CARNIVOROUS PLANTS

SORRY
ADOLF HITLER SUFFERED FROM UNCONTROLLABLE FLATULENCE

ANCIENT GREEKS BELIEVED THAT PIGEON DROPPINGS STIMULATED HAIR GROWTH

HOWARD HUGHES'S TOENAILS GREW TO ALMOST 6 INCHES LONG

ROMAN DINERS
REGULARLY VOMITED
AT THE TABLE

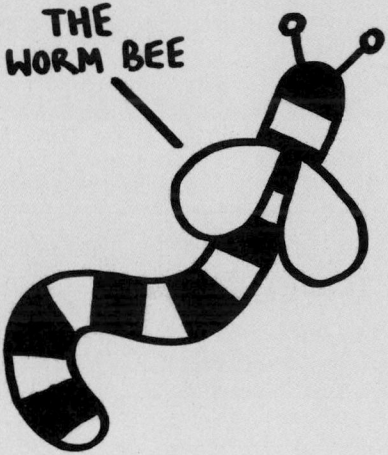

AROUND
10,000
NEW INSECTS
ARE DISCOVERED
EVERY YEAR

A MOCKINGBIRD CAN IMITATE THE SONGS OF 40 DIFFERENT BIRDS

AN ADULT MAN'S BODY CONTAINS 1.5 GALLONS OF BLOOD

THE LONGEST TAPEWORM EVER FOUND IN THE HUMAN BODY WAS 102 FEET LONG

WOODPECKERS SLAM THEIR HEADS INTO TREES AT A RATE OF 20 PECKS A SECOND

SHEEP CAN RECOGNIZE OTHER SHEEP FROM PHOTOGRAPHS

THE LARGEST KNOWN FROG IS THE GOLIATH FROG, MEASURING UP TO 34.5 INCHES LONG

THE CANADIAN COCKTAIL SOURTOE CONTAINS A PRESERVED HUMAN TOE

WOMEN HAVE A BETTER SENSE OF SMELL THAN MEN

STUNTMAN EVEL KNIEVEL HOLDS THE RECORD FOR THE MOST BROKEN BONES - 35

STANDING
FOR AN
HOUR
BURNS
120
CALORIES
6

THE
ART
OF
WRITING IS AT ITS BEST
AT 19 YEARS OLD

SOME PERFUMES CONTAIN WHALE VOMIT

GEORGE W. BUSH WAS A SCHOOL CHEERLEADER

MORE
THAN 67%
OF AMERICANS
ARE CONSIDERED
OVERWEIGHT

THE OLDEST
LIVING TREE
IS 10,000
YEARS OLD

THE LONGEST CAR
IS 100 FEET LONG

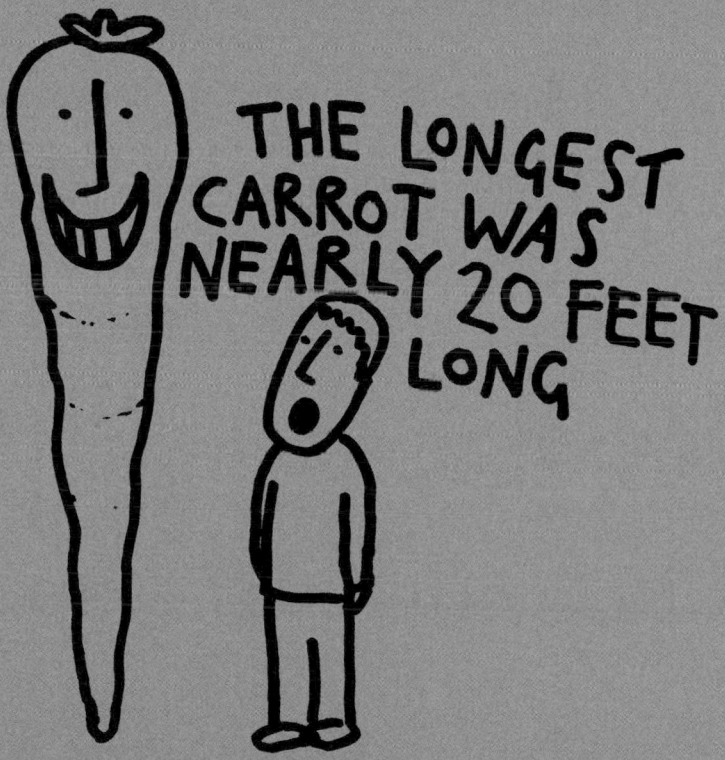
THE LONGEST CARROT WAS NEARLY 20 FEET LONG

THE BIGGEST NOSE WAS 17.5 INCHES LONG

SHARKS HAVE THE BEST SENSE OF SMELL OF ANY FISH

THE FIRST EMAIL MESSAGE WAS

THE FIRST LIVING EARTHLING IN SPACE WAS A DOG

FRANCE
IS THE MOST
POPULAR TOURIST
DESTINATION

THE FIRST MAN TO HAVE FLOWN WAS FRENCH

THE LONGEST MUSTACHE WAS 11.5 FEET LONG

AN ALBATROSS CAN
FLY NONSTOP
FOR 10 YEARS

THE LAST DODO DIED IN 1681

THE WORLD'S MOST EXPENSIVE CUP OF TEA IS $127

HENRY VIII TECHNICALLY HAD 2 WIVES NOT 6

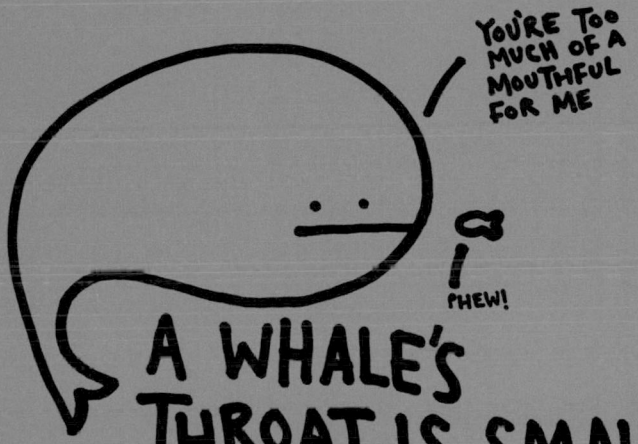

A WHALE'S THROAT IS SMALLER THAN A DINNER PLATE

BASEBALL
WAS
INVENTED
IN
ENGLAND

HELP
THE TALLEST
CAKE WAS
108 FEET
TALL

THOMAS EDISON INVENTED THE WORD "HELLO"

THE MOON
SMELLS LIKE
GUNPOWDER
BOOM

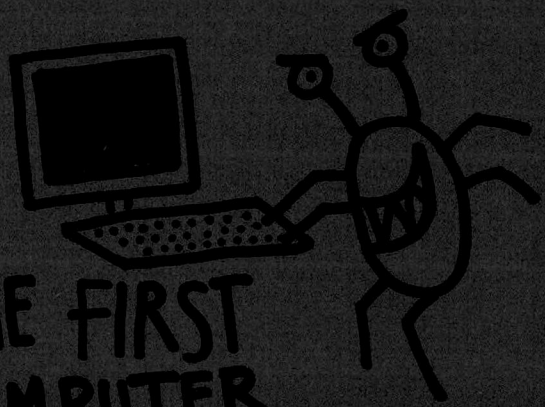

THE FIRST COMPUTER BUG WAS A REAL BUG

THE LONGEST BEARD ON A WOMAN WAS 14 INCHES LONG

THE BEACH BOYS' DENNIS WILSON DROWNED

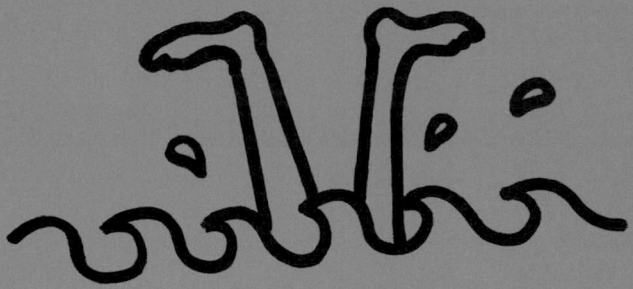

THE LOUDEST
BURP WAS 107.1 dB
(AS LOUD
AS A CHAINSAW)

THE WORLD'S OLDEST MAN WAS 138

PICASSO'S FULL NAME WAS:

PABLO DIEGO JOSÉ FRANCISCO
DE PAULA JUAN NEPOMUCENO
MARÍA DE LOS REMEDIOS
CIPRIANO DE LA SANTISIMA
TRINIDAD RUIZ Y PICASSO.

THE FASTEST
A HUMAN
MOVED
24,791
MILES
AN HOUR

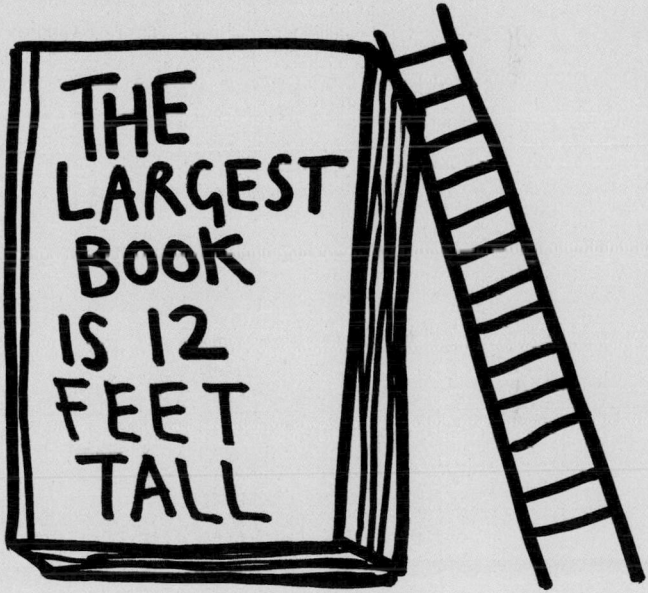
THE
LARGEST
BOOK
IS 12
FEET
TALL

THE LONGEST
HOT DOG WAS 375 FEET LONG

THE MOST EXPENSIVE CAR LICENSE PLATE IS

THE NUMBER ONE

THE TALLEST MAN EVER WAS NEARLY 9 FEET TALL

YOU HAVE
NO MUSCLES IN
YOUR FINGERS

GORILLAS
SLEEP
IN NESTS
?

TIME FLIES UNLESS YOU'RE A PIGEON
PIGEONS SEE IN SLOW MOTION

RATS
EAT 20% OF
THE WORLD'S
FOOD
SUPPLY

THE CARNIVOROUS POLAR BEAR LOVES TOOTHPASTE

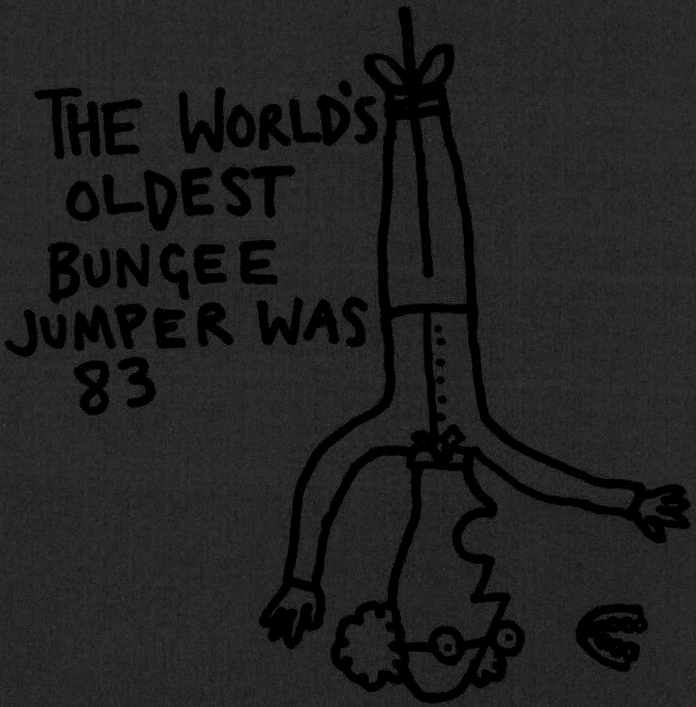
THE WORLD'S
OLDEST
BUNGEE
JUMPER WAS
83

A HIPPO
HAS THE
LARGEST
MOUTH
OF ALL
LAND
ANIMALS

THE MOST PEOPLE CRAMMED INTO A MINI IS 21

THE FIRST GAMESHOW WAS A SPELLING BEE

A 76-
YEAR-OLD
MAN
CLIMBED
MOUNT
EVEREST

THERE ARE TWICE AS MANY PEOPLE ALIVE TODAY AS IN 1960

A CHAMELEON'S CHANGING
COLOR ISN'T CAMOUFLAGE—
IT'S COMMUNICATION

THE DEADLIEST
SPIDER IS THE
BANANA SPIDER

LOOT
THE GREATEST AMOUNT STOLEN FROM A BANK IS $71.3 MILLION

THE HIGHEST
WAVE ON
RECORD IS
1,719 FEET
HIGH

IT WASN'T ME
PARP
THE LARGEST WHOOPEE CUSHION IS NEARLY 10 FEET AROUND

THE LARGEST SQUIRREL CAN GROW TO 3 FEET TALL

ROMANS WHO DISCOVERED PARROTS TAUGHT THEM TO SAY "HAIL CAESAR!"

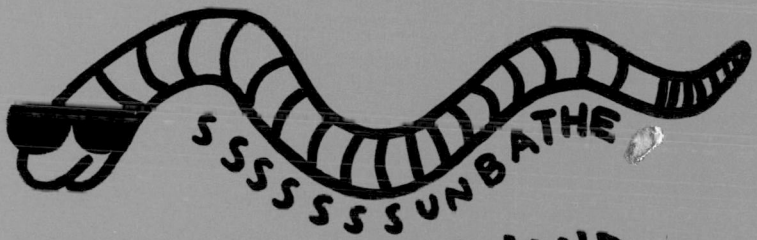

SNAKES ARE AVID SUNBATHERS

THE MOST POPULAR
JAMES BOND
THE BEST
IS SEAN
CONNERY

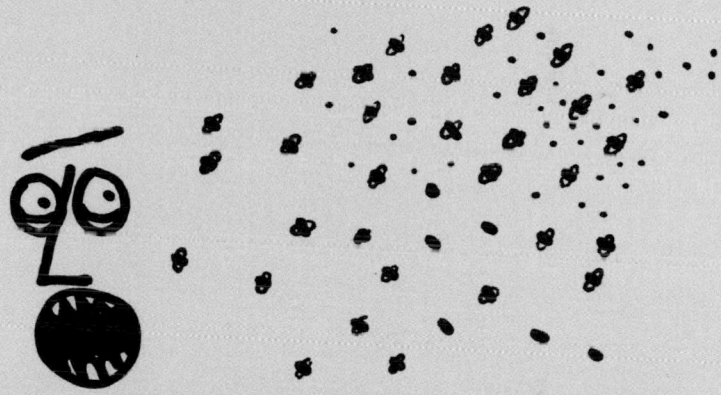

2 FLIES CAN PRODUCE
191,010,000,000,000,000,000
OFFSPRING IN 4 MONTHS

A LION'S LIFE EXPECTANCY IS SHORTER THAN THE ANTELOPE IT CHASES

HORSES
CAN
SLEEP
STANDING
UP

THE OLDEST CREATURE WAS A 255-YEAR-OLD TORTOISE

PEOPLE ARE TALLER IN THE MORNING THAN AT NIGHT

THERE ARE MORE

IN THE WORLD THAN ANY OTHER CREATURE

A WHALE'S HEART IS AS BIG AS A CAR

OSCAR WILDE'S LAST WORDS WERE "EITHER THE WALLPAPER GOES OR I DO"

CHOCOLATE IS POISONOUS TO PARROTS

A CHICKEN CAN LAY MORE THAN 200 EGGS IN A YEAR

SOME FISH
GET
SEASICK

THE AVERAGE BEEHIVE HAS 40-45,000 BEES INSIDE

THE FIRST 5 TARZAN FILMS WERE SILENT

THE LIGHT OF 6 LARGE FIREFLIES IS ENOUGH TO READ BY

STRAWBERRIES CONTAIN MORE VITAMIN C THAN ORANGES

A HIPPOPOTAMUS CAN EAT 88 POUNDS OF SOFT GRASS A DAY

THE CALL OF A BLUE WHALE IS LOUDER THAN A JUMBO JET

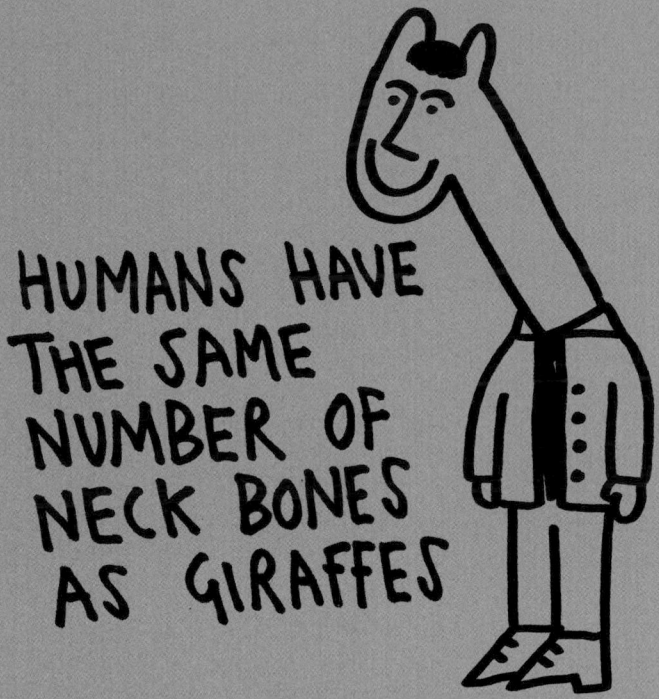
HUMANS HAVE
THE SAME
NUMBER OF
NECK BONES
AS GIRAFFES

A SINGLE STRAND OF HAIR CAN STAY ON YOUR HEAD FOR 5 YEARS

85% OF PEOPLE CAN CURL THEIR TONGUE

EATING
RED PEPPERS
TURNS
CANARIES
ORANGE

YOU CAN SMELL A SKUNK'S ODOR 2 MILES AWAY

THE QUEEN OF ENGLAND OWNS A RUBBER DUCK WEARING A CROWN

75% OF PEOPLE WEAR THE WRONG SIZE SHOES

THERE ARE AN ESTIMATED

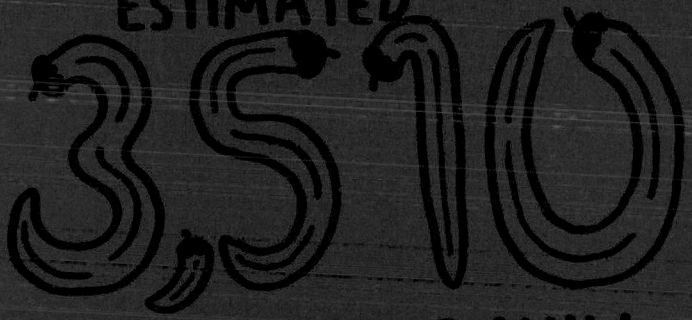

VARIATIONS OF CHILI PEPPERS

THE OLDEST GOLDFISH WAS 43

2 MILLION PEOPLE DIE EVERY YEAR FROM WORK-RELATED ACCIDENTS

DEER HAVE
INFRARED
VISION

EATING 2·2 POUNDS OF POTATOES IN ONE SITTING WILL KILL YOU

A BASKETBALL-SIZED OCTOPUS CAN FIT INTO A SODA CAN

THE HEAVIEST CAT WEIGHED 47 POUNDS

INSECT
BLOOD
IS YELLOW

AFTER MATING, THE FEMALE BLACK WIDOW EATS THE MALE

YOU ARE MORE LIKELY TO BE KILLED BY AN ASTEROID THAN BY LIGHTNING

BEETHOVEN WAS ONCE ARRESTED FOR LOOKING LIKE A TRAMP

A BABY ROBIN EATS AROUND 13 FEET OF EARTHWORMS A DAY

IN 2007,
A 4-LEGGED
DUCK WAS
BORN

YOU ARE TWICE AS LIKELY TO BE BITTEN BY A DOG DURING A FULL MOON

BEN & JERRY'S
ICE CREAM
WASTE IS
FED TO PIGS

YOU CAN
HYPNOTIZE
A CHICKEN

THE WETTEST PLACE ON EARTH IS THE INDIAN TOWN CHERRAPUNJI

A PARROT NAMED PUCK HAS A VOCABULARY OF 1,728 WORDS

THERE ARE 240 DOTS IN A PAC-MAN GAME

THERE ARE MORE MEN THAN WOMEN

THE PLASTIC BIT AT THE END OF SHOELACES IS CALLED AN AGLET

I'M THIRSTY
JELLYFISH ARE 95% WATER

FISH CAN DROWN

BEETLES DON'T LIKE HEAVY METAL MUSIC

THE WORD "ROBOT" COMES FROM THE WORD "SLAVE"

THE SUN IS
4·5 BILLION
YEARS OLD

A HUGELY INACCURATE "DAILY MIRROR" HEADLINE READ...

A QUARTER OF ALL FORESTS ARE IN RUSSIA

THE RECORD FOR HOLDING THE BREATH UNDER WATER IS 9 MINUTES, 8 SECONDS

THE FIRST
ROBOT WAS
A DUCK

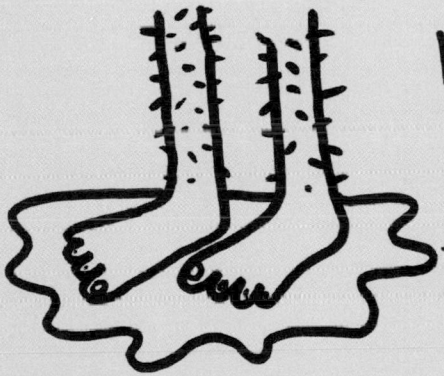

IF YOU WEE IN THE SHOWER INSTEAD OF FLUSHING A TOILET, YOU COULD SAVE 1,157 GALLONS OF WATER A YEAR

THE AVERAGE CHOCOLATE BAR HAS 8 INSECT LEGS IN IT

A BOLT OF LIGHTNING HAS ENOUGH ENERGY TO TOAST 160,000 PIECES OF BREAD

THE HAPPY BIRTHDAY SONG IS COPYRIGHTED TILL 2030
♩ HAPPY ♪ BIRTHDAY TO ME... ♫
YOU OWE MONEY

HULK HOGAN'S REAL NAME IS TERRY

ROMANS USED TO CLEAN THEIR TEETH WITH...

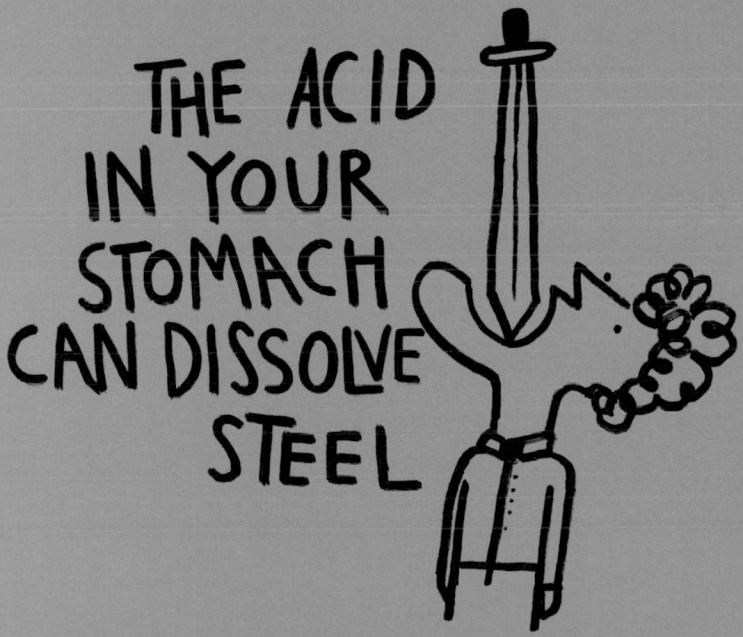
THE ACID
IN YOUR
STOMACH
CAN DISSOLVE
STEEL

OYSTERS CAN
CHANGE GENDER

ANTS HAVE THE BIGGEST BRAINS IN PROPORTION TO THEIR BODIES

IN 1314,
KING
EDWARD II
BANNED
SOCCER
IN ENGLAND

ORIGINALLY BRIDES CARRIED WEDDING FLOWERS TO MASK BODY ODOR

A MAN SURVIVED A 6.5-MILE DROP FROM A PLANE

BULLS ARE
COLOR-BLIND

MONDAY THE 27TH IS STATISTICALLY MORE UNLUCKY THAN FRIDAY THE 13TH

FLIES
BEAT
THEIR
WINGS 180
TIMES A SECOND

AROUND
250 PEOPLE
HAVE DIED AFTER
FALLING FROM
THE LEANING
TOWER OF PISA

BEING CRUSHED BY AN ELEPHANT WAS A POPULAR FORM OF EXECUTION IN ASIA

GANGSTER
AL CAPONE'S
BUSINESS
CARD READ...
AL CAPONE
FURNITURE
DEALER

THE MOST POWERFUL MUSCLE IN YOUR BODY IS USED FOR CHEWING

THE LOUDEST SNORE RECORDED WAS 93 DECIBELS— LOUDER THAN A CAR ENGINE

3,000-YEAR-OLD MUMMIES STILL HAVE THEIR FINGER-PRINTS

THE LARGEST LIVING THING IS A MUSHROOM

YOUR EYES MAKE 1.2 GALLONS OF TEARS A YEAR

IF YOUR HEAD IS CUT OFF YOU CAN REMAIN CONSCIOUS FOR 25 SECONDS

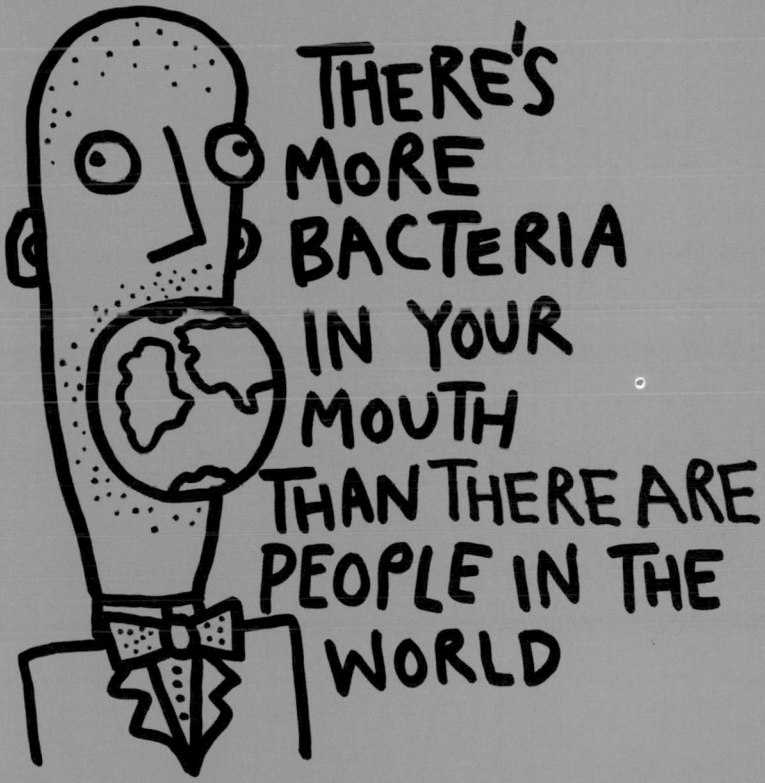
THERE'S
MORE
BACTERIA
IN YOUR
MOUTH
THAN THERE ARE
PEOPLE IN THE
WORLD

EATING
TOO MANY
CARROTS
WILL
TURN YOU
ORANGE

THE SMALLEST ADULT PERSON WAS 22·5 INCHES TALL

IN 1740, A COW WAS ACCUSED OF BEING A WITCH AND KILLED

RUDOLPH THE REINDEER IS A FEMALE

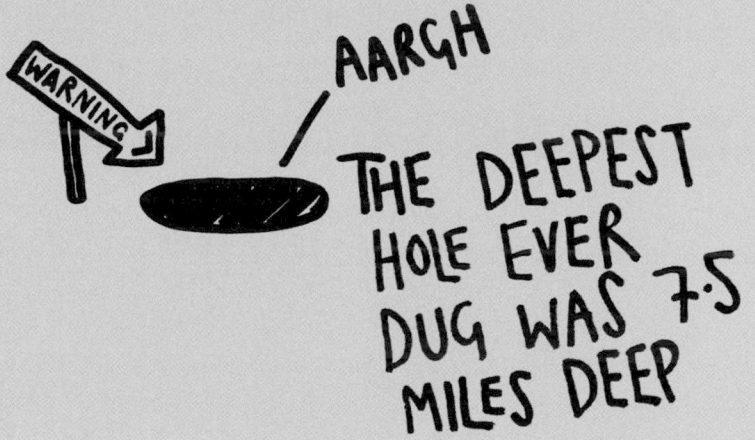
WARNING
AARGH
THE DEEPEST HOLE EVER DUG WAS 7.5 MILES DEEP

LISTEN. I'M SORRY ABOUT EVERYTHING
THERE ARE MORE CHICKENS ON THE EARTH THAN PEOPLE

THE MOST COMMON LIE IS
I'M FINE!

IF YOU MULTIPLY
111,111,111
BY
111,111,111
YOU GET
12,345,678,987,654,321

MORE PEOPLE HAVE HEART ATTACKS ON MONDAYS THAN ON OTHER DAYS OF THE WEEK

A CATERPILLAR HAS
MORE MUSCLES
THAN YOU DO

KING LOUIS XVI, VICTIM OF THE GUILLOTINE, HELPED DESIGN IT

MORE PEOPLE ARE BORN IN AUGUST THAN ANY OTHER MONTH

"STAR TREK" CREATOR GENE RODDENBERRY HAD THE FIRST SPACE FUNERAL

HELP
EVERY DAY
AT LEAST ONE
VOLCANO IS
ERUPTING

YOU NEED A HAIRCUT
HAIR GROWS FASTER IN SUMMER

SPANISH IS MORE WIDELY SPOKEN THAN ENGLISH

AN ANAGRAM OF ALBERT EINSTEIN IS TEN ELITE BRAINS

WE ARE TECHNICALLY
STILL IN
AN ICE AGE

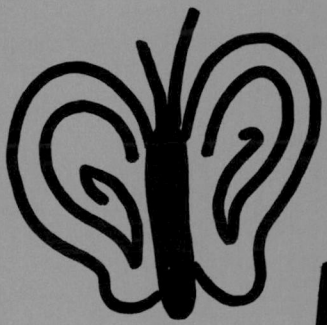

BUTTERFLIES HAVE GREAT HEARING

THERE ARE
3 TOWNS IN
AMERICA
CALLED
SANTA CLAUS

THE WORLD'S LONGEST RUNNING PLAY IS "MOUSETRAP"

THE FIRST WORD RECORDED WAS "MARY"

NEW YORK
USED TO BE
CALLED
NEW AMSTERDAM

THERE IS NO SUCH NUMBER AS A ZILLION

PLUTO ISN'T A PLANET

SUGAR IS THE ONLY TASTE HUMANS ARE BORN CRAVING

BETWEEN 1784 AND 1811, BRITISH MEN NEEDED A LICENSE TO WEAR A HAT

PICASSO WAS ONCE ACCUSED OF STEALING THE "MONA LISA"

PICASSO'S VERSION

THERE ARE MORE SHEEP IN THE BIBLE THAN ANY OTHER ANIMAL

MOZART
BEGAN
COMPOSING
AT AGE 5

THE RECORD FOR SNEEZING IS 2.5 YEARS

ELVIS HAD
A TWIN BROTHER

HITLER'S REAL NAME WAS SCHICKLGRUBER

HARD WORK

VITUS IS THE
PATRON SAINT
OF DOG BITES

URUGUAY USED HARD CHEESE AS CANNON-BALLS IN A WAR WITH BRAZIL

THE
STATUE
OF LIBERTY
WAS MADE
IN FRANCE

TV SOAP OPERAS ARE SO CALLED BECAUSE THEY WERE SPONSORED BY SOAP MANUFACTURERS

THE WORLD'S MOST

COMMON DISEASE

IS TOOTH DECAY

A FEMALE ELEPHANT
IS CALLED A COW

THE FIRST SONG VIDEO ON MTV WAS "VIDEO KILLED THE RADIO STAR"

THE ENGLISH INVENTED CHAMPAGNE

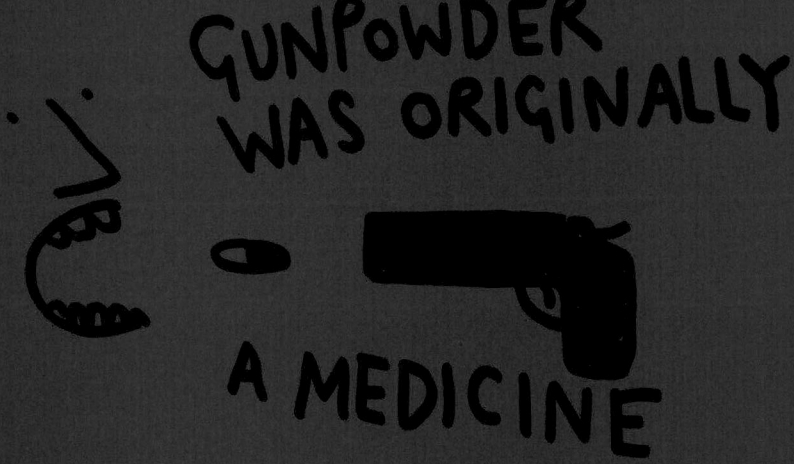
GUNPOWDER
WAS ORIGINALLY
A MEDICINE

CATS CAN SURVIVE FALLS FROM ABOVE THE 7TH FLOOR OF BUILDINGS

THE SMALLEST DOG IN THE WORLD IS 2.5 INCHES TALL

GEORGE WASHINGTON HAD FALSE TEETH MADE FROM HIPPO TEETH

A DAY ISN'T EXACTLY 24 HOURS LONG

THE WHEEL WAS
INVENTED IN THE YEAR
5000 BC

VIKINGS CLEANED THEIR BOTTOMS WITH SHEEP'S WOOL

CHARLIE CHAPLIN'S CORPSE WAS ONCE STOLEN

SOUND TRAVELS 4 TIMES FASTER IN WATER THAN IN AIR

THE MONTH OF JULY WAS NAMED AFTER JULIUS CAESAR

HENRY VI BECAME KING WHEN HE WAS 8 MONTHS OLD

THE FASTEST CREATURE IS A FALCON, REACHING 185 MPH

ON AVERAGE BRITONS EAT 11 POUNDS OF BAKED BEANS A YEAR

THE TIN CAN OPENER WAS INVENTED 50 YEARS AFTER THE TIN CAN

THE QUESTION MARK WAS INVENTED IN THE 1580s

80% OF IMAGES ON
THE INTERNET ARE PORNOGRAPHIC

NOT
THIS ONE

MOST SPIDERS HAVE 8 EYES

THERE ARE NO CLOCKS IN LAS VEGAS CASINOS

ISAAC NEWTON INVENTED THE CAT DOOR
I'VE GOT ANOTHER IDEA

IF YOU RECEIVED ALL OF THE GIFTS
IN THE SONG "12 DAYS OF CHRISTMAS"
YOU WOULD RECEIVE 364 PRESENTS

THE LONGEST FART RECORDED LASTED 2 MINUTES, 42 SECONDS

THE LARGEST
MAN-MADE
STRUCTURE
IS A TRASH
DUMP IN
NEW YORK

THE WORLD'S OLDEST LIGHTBULB HASN'T BEEN TURNED OFF SINCE 1901

IT IS LEGAL TO MARRY A DEAD PERSON IN FRANCE

THE AVERAGE PENCIL CAN DRAW A 35-MILE-LONG LINE

ALEXANDER GRAHAM BELL, THE INVENTOR OF THE TELEPHONE, COULDN'T CALL HIS WIFE...

SHE WAS DEAF

GETH WOULD LIKE TO THANK PETE

PETE WOULD LIKE TO THANK GETH

AND WE WOULD BOTH LIKE TO
THANK EVERYONE THAT HAS
HELPED ALONG THE WAY...

"LEARN SOMETHING EVERY DAY" IS A SELF-INITIATED PROJECT
BY YOUNG · YOUNG IS A CREATIVE AGENCY BASED IN THE U.K.
FOUNDED BY PETER JARVIS AND GETHIN VAUGHAN.
WWW.LEARNSOMETHINGEVERYDAY.CO.UK
WWW.WEAREYOUNG.CO.UK